LET'S BE
EARLY SETTLERS
with
DANIEL BOONE

by PEGGY PARISH
Drawings by Arnold Lobel

HARPER & ROW, PUBLISHERS
New York, Evanston, and London

FOR
JANE BEEBE
MARTHA CAHN
VICKI EDELMAN
LIZ FELDMAN
WIN HOOVER
LEONA JAGLOM
JOSH NEUBAUER
JULIE RUBEN
PEGGY STERN
KATHY TROWBRIDGE
ANDY BRENNER
PETER di BONAVENTURA
KRISTIN ELIASBERG
QUINA FONSECA
CHARLES HYLE
SAM MARSHALL
ALISON READ
NOAH SEAMAN
TOBY TRAGER
DREW WILDER

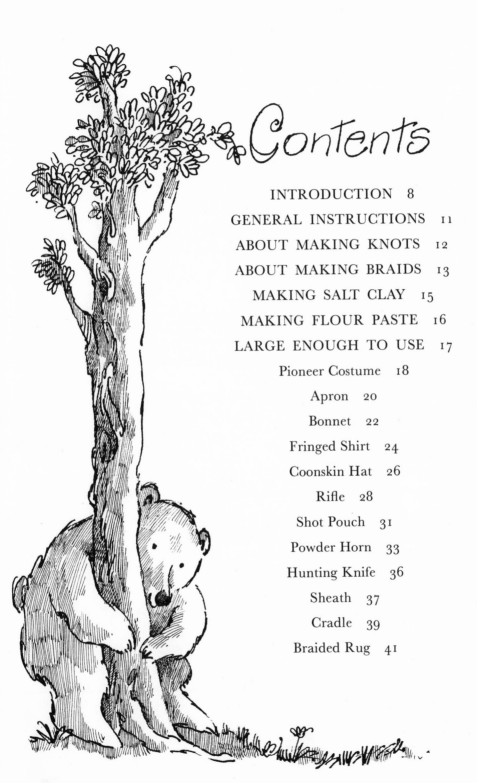

Contents

It was many years after our country was discovered before white men came here to live. The first settlers came from across the Atlantic Ocean. Some came for adventure, some came for freedom, and some came to make money. But they all found a great land covered with forests. And they all found much hard work.

There were no stores to sell them what they needed. They had brought a few things with them. But the rest they had to make for themselves. Life was not easy in those early days. It took a lot of courage and much, much hard work just to make a living.

Daniel Boone was an early settler. He was born in Pennsylvania in 1734. Later he and his family moved to North Carolina.

Daniel Boone was always hearing of the wonderful land across the mountains. Being a man of adventure, he felt he must explore it. He and a small group of men blazed a trail through the wilderness. Daniel Boone liked the richness of the soil and the ample supply of game he found. In 1775 he started the settlement of Boonesboro in what is now the state of Kentucky.

Daniel Boone died in 1820. He was a great man and spent his life in helping our country grow into the wonderful land it is today.

This book will tell you a little about the early settlers' way of life and the kinds of things they used in the days of Daniel Boone. Some of the things are large enough to use for giving plays or in pretend games. Some are small models with which you can make dioramas. Others are just for fun.

General Instructions

For the best results with these projects you should

1. Read and follow the instructions carefully.

2. Use a good all-purpose glue (Elmer's Glue-All, Sobo).

3. Use tempera paints. (These can be purchased at any stationery or dime store.)

4. Add a little liquid soap to the paint if you are going to paint a waxed or glossy surface or over tape.

5. When painting cotton, thin the paint with water and pat the paint on with the brush.

6. Always wash your paint brush thoroughly before you change to another color.

About Making Knots

For many of these projects rather large, tight knots are needed.

To make a knot:

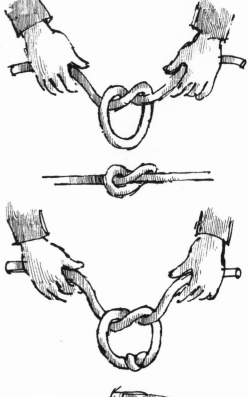

1. Loop one end of the thread over, around, and under the thread.

2. Pull the ends of the thread to draw the loop into a knot.

3. Make another loop the same way.

4. Pull the second loop into a knot on top of the first.

About Making Braids

Some of the projects call for braiding. The pictures will show you how to do this.

1. Divide the material into three parts as nearly equal as possible.

2. Bring an outside piece across the middle piece.

3. Bring the opposite outside piece across the middle piece.

4. Continue bringing out-side pieces over the middle piece, working from first one side and then the other, until you have al-most reached the end. Then tie the ends together with a small piece of string.

Making Salt Clay

Salt clay is used for a number of projects. Salt clay keeps well. It can be stored in a plastic bag. If the clay becomes sticky after being stored, just add a little more flour. Salt clay objects need time to dry. They will dry faster if placed near heat.

To make salt clay:

1. Mix one cup of flour with one cup of salt.

2. Add a little cool water and mix with your hands. If the mixture is too dry, add a little more water.

3. Mix until you have a ball of clay. This clay should be firm and not at all sticky. If it is sticky, add more flour.

Making Flour Paste

Several of the projects call for flour paste.
To make flour paste:

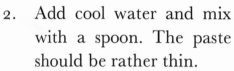

1. Put some flour in a bowl
   or pan.

2. Add cool water and mix
   with a spoon. The paste
   should be rather thin.

3. If the paste thickens before you have finished your
   project, just add more
   water and mix it well.

Large Enough to Use

Pioneer Costume

The early settlers did not get new clothes very often. The women had to make everything the family wore. But before they could make anything, they must first spin thread. Then they must weave the thread into cloth. The favorite cloth was linsey-woolsey. This is linen and wool woven together. The strong linen threads made the wool last longer.

Using an old sheet, you can make a fun costume in the same style as the early settlers wore. For a pattern, girls may use a loose-fitting bathrobe or nightgown. Boys may use a loose-fitting pajama coat or a bathrobe and cut the costume a little shorter than the robe.

Boys and girls follow the same instructions through step 5.

1. Double the cloth and lay it flat. Lay the pattern (buttoned up) on the sheet so that the shoulder seams are on the fold and the sleeves are straight out. With a pencil, mark where the hole for your head should be.

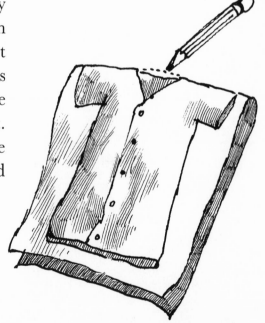

2. The sleeves of your pattern may not be exactly on the fold, but pretend that they are and draw the rest of the pattern.

3. Remove the pattern and cut along the lines. Be sure to cut through both layers of cloth.

4. Sew the bottoms of the sleeves and both sides of the costume.

5. Turn the costume so that the seams are on the inside.

Boys see "Fringed Shirt," p. 24.

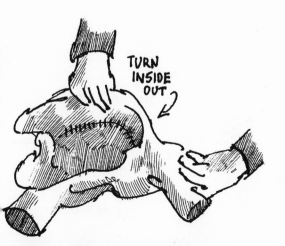

TURN INSIDE OUT

Women and girls wore very simple long dresses. You can use your costume as it is for the dress part. If the hole for your head is not large enough, cut a slit in the middle of the back. This can be pinned when you wear the costume.

Apron

But women and girls always wore an apron over their dresses.

To make an apron:

1. Cut a wide strip of cloth long enough to fit loosely around you.

2. Turn under a two-inch hem across the top to make a casing for a drawstring. Sew the hem down. Stitch close to the inside edge.

3. Cut a strip of cloth about two inches wide and long enough to go around your waist twice for use as a drawstring.

2 INCHES

4. Fold the strip in half at one end and pin it with a large safety pin. Stick the closed safety pin into the casing and thread the drawstring through.

5. Remove the safety pin. Pull the apron along the drawstring until it is the way you want it. Put the apron on and tie the drawstring into a bow.

Bonnet

Women and girls almost always wore a bonnet, too.

1. To make the pattern for your bonnet, cut a piece of newspaper about ten inches wide and long enough to go around your head with an inch left over. Round off the corners at one end as shown in the picture.

2. Double a piece of cloth. Lay the pattern on it. Draw around the pattern.

3. Remove the pattern and cut along the lines. Be sure to cut through both layers of cloth.

10 INCHES

4. Put the two pieces together. The straight edge will be the back of the bonnet. Starting about an inch from the center of the back, sew the pieces together. Leave an opening in the center of the back for turning. Turn the bonnet so that the seams are on the inside. Sew the opening.

5. Fit the bonnet around your head. Sew or staple the ends in place.

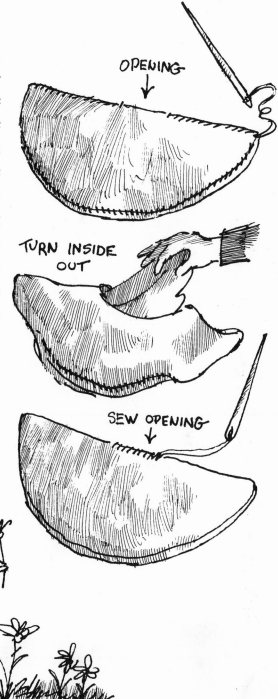

OPENING

TURN INSIDE OUT

SEW OPENING

Fringed Shirt

Men and boys liked to wear fringed shirts. They were usually made of linsey-woolsey and were open down the front.

To make a fringed shirt:

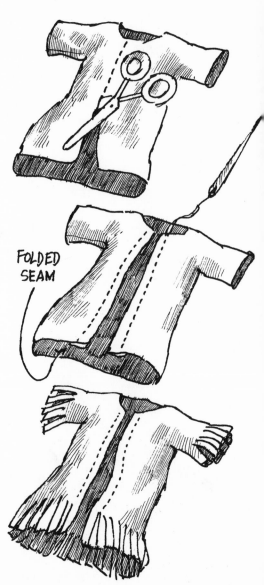

1. Lay the costume flat. Draw a line down the middle of the front. Cut along this line. Be careful not to cut the back.

2. Turn under a one-inch hem on each side of the front. Sew the hem down.

   FOLDED SEAM

3. Cut slits around the ends of the sleeves and the bottom of the shirt to make fringes.

4. Cut a strip of cloth about five inches wide and twice the length of your shirt. Cut slits in the cloth to within an inch from one edge.

5. Starting at one side of the front opening, a few inches below the neck, sew on the fringe across the front and over the shoulders as shown in the picture.

6. You may want to dye your shirt. You can make the dye yourself. (See "Making Dyes," page 61.)

5 INCHES

SEW HERE

SEW HERE

Coonskin Hat

The fashion in headwear for men and boys was a coonskin hat. Of course you can't make a real one without a real raccoon skin, but you can make a pretend one.

1. Cut a strip of lightweight cardboard long enough to go around your head with two inches left over.

2. Fit the band around your head, then staple or tape the ends in place.

STAPLE OR TAPE

3. Place this cardboard band on a piece of cloth and draw a slightly larger circle around it. Cut this out.

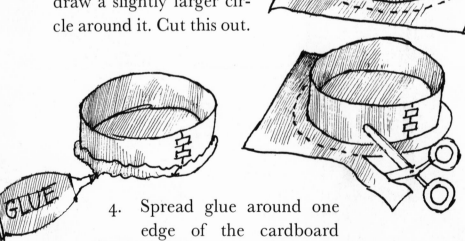

GLUE

4. Spread glue around one edge of the cardboard band.

5. Lay the cloth circle flat and place the cardboard band, with the glued side down, in the center. Pull the edge of the cloth over the cardboard and press it onto the glue. This makes the frame for the hat.

6. Cut the coonskin tail the size and shape you want it from a piece of cloth. Glue the tail in place at the lower edge of the cardboard band. Let the glue dry.

7. Spread glue over the frame and cover it with cotton. Then do the same with the tail. Let the glue dry.

8. Paint over the cotton. Be sure to paint stripes on the tail. Let the paint dry.

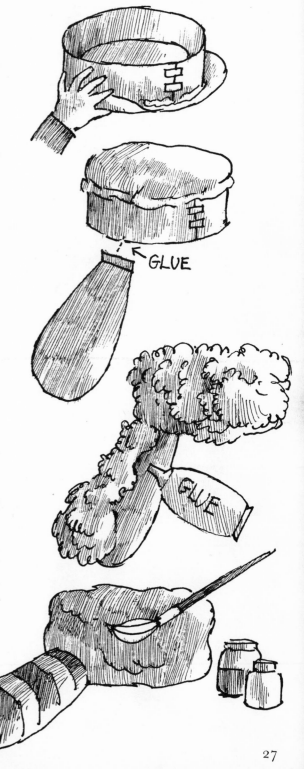

Rifle

A rifle was a man's steady companion. He never knew what kinds of dangers he might meet. And without a rifle he could not kill the animals he must have for food for his family. Some men even gave their guns a name. Daniel Boone called his Tick-Licker.

1. To make the barrel of your rifle, open two sheets of newspaper to their full size. Starting from a long side, roll the papers into a tight tube. Tape the edges in place.

2. For the handle, cut two pieces of cardboard twelve inches long and three inches wide. Shape the

cardboard as shown in the picture. Glue a piece of cardboard on each side of the barrel, starting about six inches from one end. Let the glue dry.

3. Crumple up newspaper and pad the empty spaces between the cardboard. Tape the paper in place.

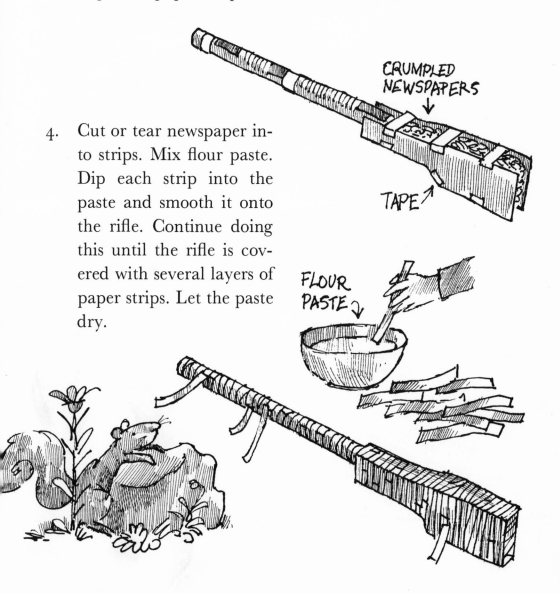

CRUMPLED NEWSPAPERS ↓

TAPE ↗

4. Cut or tear newspaper into strips. Mix flour paste. Dip each strip into the paste and smooth it onto the rifle. Continue doing this until the rifle is covered with several layers of paper strips. Let the paste dry.

FLOUR PASTE ↓

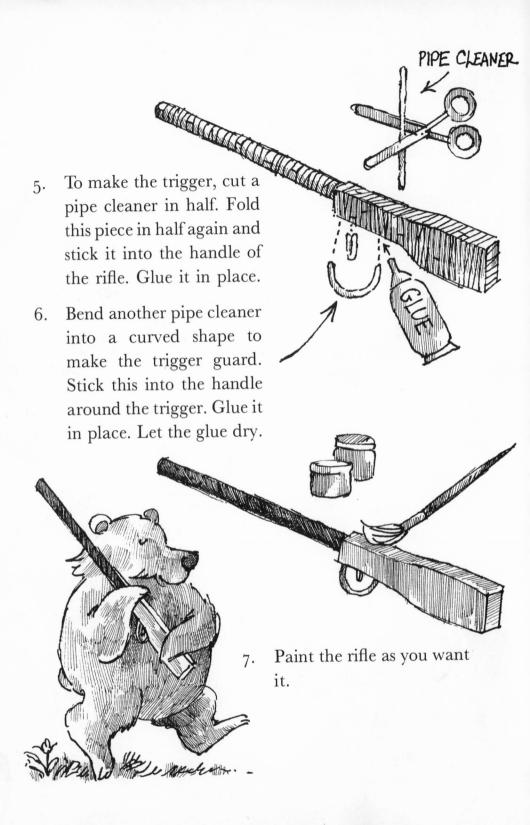

5. To make the trigger, cut a pipe cleaner in half. Fold this piece in half again and stick it into the handle of the rifle. Glue it in place.

6. Bend another pipe cleaner into a curved shape to make the trigger guard. Stick this into the handle around the trigger. Glue it in place. Let the glue dry.

7. Paint the rifle as you want it.

Shot Pouch

A man also had his leather shot pouch with him most of the time. In this he carried lead for making bullets, a bullet mold, the flint and steel with which to start fire, and some lead rifle balls.

1. To make your pattern for a shot pouch, cut a piece of newspaper fourteen inches wide and nine inches deep. Round off the corners at one end as shown in the picture.

2. Double a piece of cloth and lay the pattern, with the straight edge along the fold, on it. With a pencil draw around the pattern.

3. Remove the pattern and cut along the lines. Be sure to cut through both layers of cloth.

4. Double another piece of cloth and lay the straight edge of the pattern four inches below the fold. (The extra piece will make the flap for the pouch.) Draw around the pattern, making the line come straight from the fold to the pattern. Remove the pattern and cut along the lines.

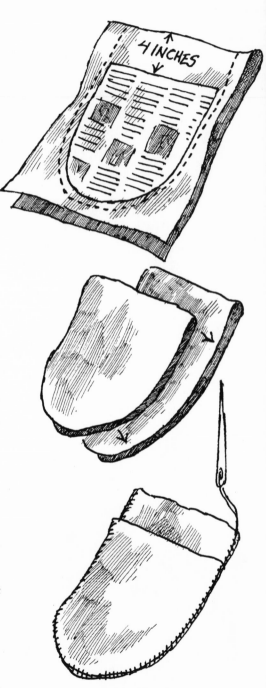

5. Put all four pieces of cloth together, making them fit at the rounded edges. Starting at the top fold, sew the pieces together all the way around.

6. Turn the pouch so that the seams will be inside. The flap seams will be outside.

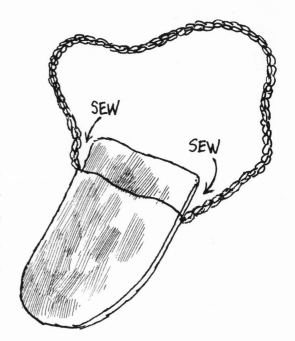

7. Paint the pouch brown. Let the paint dry.

8. Braid a strap long enough to reach across your shoulders and to the opposite side of your waist. Sew an end of the strap to each side of the pouch.

Powder Horn

A man's powder horn was made from the horn of a cow or a buffalo. In this he carried his gunpowder.

To make a powder horn:

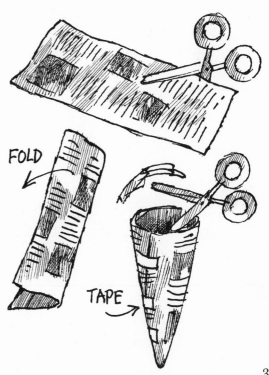

1. Cut a sheet of newspaper in half the long way. Then fold it in half the same way. Starting with a corner on the folded edge, roll the paper into a cone shape. Tape the edges in place.

2. Trim the top evenly all the way around. Tape all loose edges.

NEWSPAPERS

FLOUR PASTE

3. Stuff the horn with newspaper so it will hold its shape.

4. Mix a flour paste. Cut or tear newspaper into strips. Dip each strip into the flour paste and smooth it onto the horn. Continue doing this until the horn is covered with several layers of strips. Curve the point of the horn with paste strips. Let the paste dry. Remove the newspaper stuffing.

5. Cut a circle of cardboard large enough to cover the open end of the horn. Tape the cover to the horn on one side only, so you can open and close it.

6. Cut two pieces of string, each eight inches long. Glue one piece to each end of the horn. Paint the horn. Let the paint dry.

7. Lay the powder horn across the front of the shot pouch. Tie a string to each side of the strap of the pouch.

Hunting Knife

A hunting knife was another prized and important possession for a man. When he went on long hunting trips he had to have a knife to skin animals and cut up the meat.

To make a pretend knife:

1. On a piece of cardboard draw a form as shown in the picture the size you want your knife to be. Cut the shape out.

2. Draw a line across the straight end of the form where you want the handle to end. Lay the form on a piece of cardboard and draw around the handle. Cut this out. Make two of these. Glue one to each side of the frame.

3. Cut or tear newspaper into strips. Mix flour paste. Dip each strip into the paste and smooth it onto the knife.

GLUE

FLOUR PASTE

Continue doing this until the knife is covered with several layers of paper strips. Let the paste dry and paint the knife.

Sheath

The hunting knife was carried in a sheath. The man wore his sheath on a belt or tied around his waist. You may want to make a sheath for your knife.

1. Fold a piece of cloth. Lay the knife on the cloth so that the handle is partly above the fold.

2. Draw a line about a half inch from the blade all around it. Remove the knife and cut along the lines. Make two sets of these.

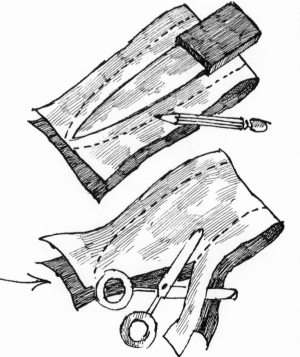

3. Put the pieces of cloth together. Starting at the top fold sew the pieces together all the way around to the top fold on the other side.

4. Turn the sheath so that the seams will be inside.

5. Cut a strip of cloth about one inch wide and six inches long. Fold the strip in half. Sew the strip to the top fold of one side of the sheath to make a belt loop.

6. Paint the sheath. Let the paint dry.

7. You may wear the sheath on a belt or tear a strip of cloth long enough to go around your waist and tie it on.

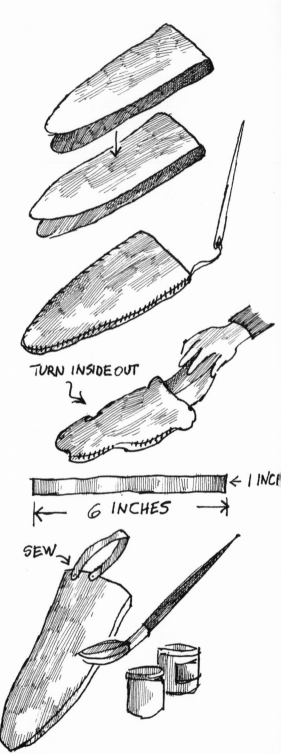

TURN INSIDE OUT

← 1 INCH

6 INCHES

SEW

Cradle

A baby's cradle was often made by hollowing out half of a log and pegging on the end pieces. The father used the Indian method to hollow out the log. First he put hot coals on the wood and let them char it. Then he scraped away the charred part. He continued doing this until the cradle was the way he wanted it. The early settlers also made buckets, barrels, and bowls in this way.

A cradle was the best kind of bed for an early settler's baby. The busy mother could keep it close by and rock it with her foot while she used her hands for other work.

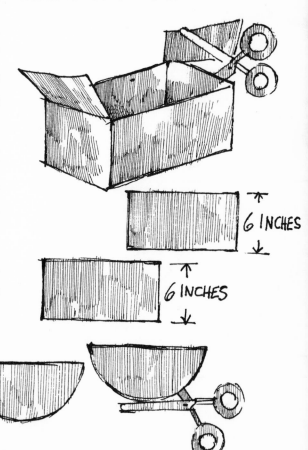

1. Find a cardboard carton the size you want your cradle to be. Cut the flaps off and trim the edges evenly all the way around.

2. Cut two pieces of cardboard a little wider than the end of the box and about six inches deep.

6 INCHES

6 INCHES

3. Round off the sides and bottom of each piece to make the rockers.

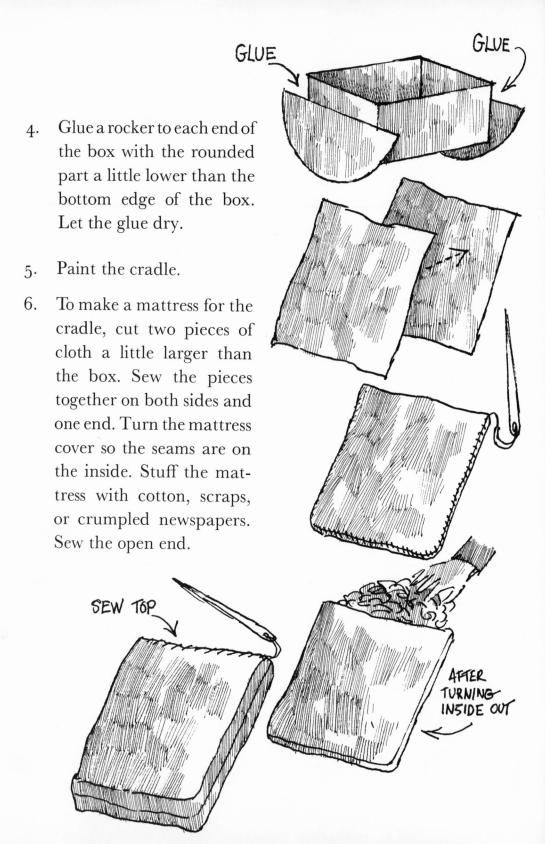

GLUE   GLUE

4. Glue a rocker to each end of the box with the rounded part a little lower than the bottom edge of the box. Let the glue dry.

5. Paint the cradle.

6. To make a mattress for the cradle, cut two pieces of cloth a little larger than the box. Sew the pieces together on both sides and one end. Turn the mattress cover so the seams are on the inside. Stuff the mattress with cotton, scraps, or crumpled newspapers. Sew the open end.

SEW TOP

AFTER TURNING INSIDE OUT

Braided Rug

Worn-out clothing and cloth scraps can be used for making braided rugs.

You can make a braided rug for your doll house.

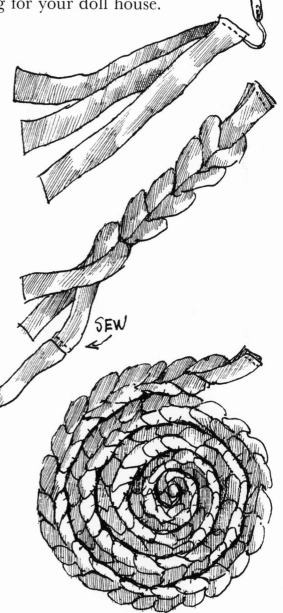

1. Cut strips of cloth about an inch wide. Select three strips and sew them together at one end.

2. Braid the strips. As the ends grow short, sew on other strips and continue braiding.

3. Thread a needle. Knot the end of the thread. Coil one end of the braid into a tight circle. Sew the coiled edges together as shown in the picture.

SEW

4. Continue coiling the braid and sewing the edges together. When you come to the end of the braid, knot the thread tightly.

Patchwork Quilt

Scraps of cloth were also saved to make patchwork quilts. A woman and her daughters sewed the scraps together to make lovely patterns. Each pattern had its own special name. There was the Log Cabin, Pandora's Box, Clam Shell, Shoo Fly, Nine Patch, Hen and Chicks, and many others. Some of these patterns are still being used today.

When the quilt top was finished, neighboring women were invited to a quilting party to help line the cover. The women spread a thin layer of wool between the quilt top and a plain linen backing. Then with tiny, tiny stitches they sewed the two together all over to hold the lining in place.

You can make a patchwork quilt for your cradle.

1. Cut scraps of cloth into squares about three inches long and three inches wide.

2. Sew the squares together to make a strip as long as your cradle. Make another strip the same length, and sew the two strips together. Continue doing this until the quilt top is as wide as you want it.

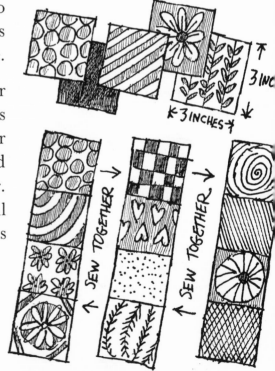

3. Cut another piece of cloth the same size as the quilt top. Put the two pieces together so that the right sides are facing each other. Sew both sides and one end together. Turn the cover so that the seams are on the inside.

4. Pad the inside of the cover with a thin layer of cotton. Then sew the open end.

5. To quilt the cover and hold the cotton in place, sew along each strip of squares, both across and up and down.

COTTON

AFTER TURNING INSIDE OUT

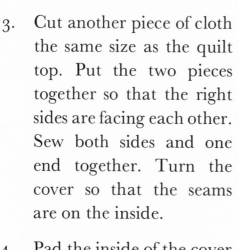

SEW

SEW

SEW

SEW

SEW

Rag Doll

Girls had their dolls in the days of the early settlers, too. But they were not like the dolls you know today. Their dolls were homemade. Some were made from corncobs. Others were made from rags.

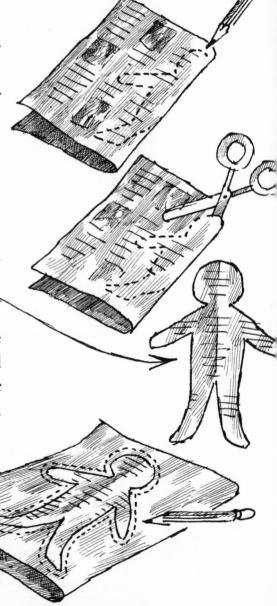

1. To make the pattern for a rag doll, fold a sheet of newspaper. Starting from the fold, draw one side of the doll the size you want it to be.

2. Cut along the lines, making sure to cut through both layers of paper. Unfold the paper and you have your pattern.

3. Double a piece of cloth. Lay the pattern on the cloth. Draw your doll slightly larger than the pattern to allow for seams.

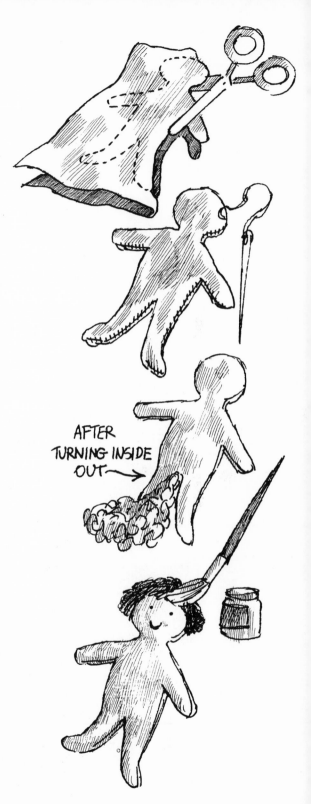

4. Remove the pattern and cut along the lines.

5. Sew the pieces together. Leave about a two-inch opening between the legs to allow for turning and stuffing.

6. Turn the doll so the seams are to the inside. Stuff the doll with cotton, scraps, or bits of crumpled newspaper. Sew up the opening.

7. Glue cotton on the doll's head where you want hair to be. Let the glue dry.

8. Paint the doll's hair and skin as you want them.

9. Glue on two small round buttons for eyes and a bit of red cloth or paper for a mouth.

AFTER TURNING INSIDE OUT→

Doll's Dress

To make a dress for your doll:

1. Double a piece of cloth so that it is wide enough to reach from the end of one arm of the doll to the end of the other arm.

2. Fold under a one-inch hem along the top of the cloth to make a casing for a drawstring. Sew the hem down, stitching close to the inside edge.

3. Bring the two side ends of the cloth together. Starting about two inches below the casing, sew the pieces together. Turn the dress so the casing hem and seam are on the inside.

AFTER TURNING INSIDE OUT

ARMHOLES

4. Fold the dress so that the seam is in the middle of the back. Just below the neckline casing cut an armhole on each side of the dress.

5. Cut a piece of ribbon or yarn about twice as long as the width of the dress to use as a drawstring. Thread the drawstring through the casing. (If you tie the drawstring to a bobby pin or a safety pin, it will be easier to slide through.)

6. Put the dress on the doll and pull the drawstring until it fits snugly around the doll's neck. Tie the drawstring in a bow.

FRONT

BACK

Broom

Splint brooms were the most popular with the early settlers. It was a man's or boy's job to do the whittling when a woman needed a new broom. The making of a good splint broom often took three evenings of whittling by the fireside.

You can make a pretend splint broom very quickly.

1. Open three sheets of newspaper to their full size. Starting from a long side, roll the papers into a tube to make the broom handle. Tape the edges in place.

2. Cut the bottoms from three large brown paper bags. Split the bags so they lie flat. Draw a line across the bags about two inches from the top.

3. Going from the bottom edge to the line, cut the bags into narrow slits. (You can cut all three bags at once.)

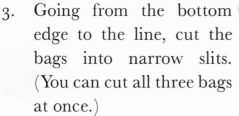

4. Wrap the bags around one end of the handle, with the strips pointing toward the other end. Tape the bags in place.

5. Turn the handle so that the strips flip down and over the end of the handle. Pull the strips together and tie them with a string to hold them in place.

Hornbook

Children did not go to school regularly. Many times there was no school near enough. Often there was so much work to be done at home their parents could not spare them.

When there was a schoolhouse, it was a log cabin. The children sat on long benches. Everybody was in one room and shared one teacher.

The youngest children learned from a hornbook. This was nothing more than a paddle-shaped board with the large and small letters of the alphabet on it. It was covered with a thin sheet of cow's horn to keep it clean.

A play hornbook is easy to make.

1. On a piece of cardboard draw a paddle shape as shown in the picture.

2. Cut a piece of white paper the same size as the wide part of the paddle.

3. Write the alphabet in capital and small letters on the white paper. Place the alphabet sheet on the paddle.

4. Cut a piece of plastic wrap a little larger than the paper. Place the plastic wrap over the alphabet sheet. Fold the edges to the back of the paddle and tape them in place.

PLASTIC WRAP

Quill Pen

Children wrote with quill pens made from feathers. The ink was blotted with sand. Turkey feathers make very good quill pens.

1. Cut the tip from a quill.

2. Split through the middle of the shaft for about a half inch. Cut away one side of the split part.

3. Sharpen the remaining side into a point.

4. Dip the point of the quill pen into some ink. Shake off the excess ink. Do not press down too hard when you write or your pen will quickly get a dull point.

5. If the point does get dull, wash off the ink and re-sharpen it.

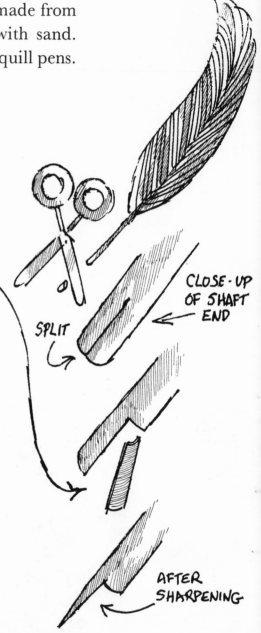

SPLIT

CLOSE-UP OF SHAFT END

AFTER SHARPENING

Dunce Cap

And if a child did not learn, he had to sit in a corner and wear a dunce cap.

You can make a dunce cap from two or three sheets of newspaper.

1. Starting with a corner on the folded edge, roll the paper into a cone shape. Tape the pointed edge in place.

2. Fit the cone on your head and tape the lower edge in place.

3. Trim the edge evenly all around. Tape all loose edges.

4. Paint the hat and let the paint dry.

TAPE

53

Sampler

It was most important for little girls to learn to sew. Often they learned their letters and sewing by making a sampler.

Even though you already know your letters, you might enjoy making a sampler.

1. Cut a piece of cloth the size you want your sampler to be.

2. With a pencil, very neatly write the letters of the alphabet on the cloth.

3. Thread a needle with two strands of embroidery cotton. Make a knot in one end.

4. Bring the needle up through the cloth at the beginning of a letter.

CLOSE-UP OF LETTER

NEEDLE →

5. With the thread to the left of the needle, insert the needle, with the point coming toward you, a short distance away on the line. Bring the needle out again on the line.

6. Continue doing this, always keeping the thread to the left of the needle, until you have completed the letter.

7. Make a knot on the underside of the cloth. Knot the thread in your needle and go on to the next letter.

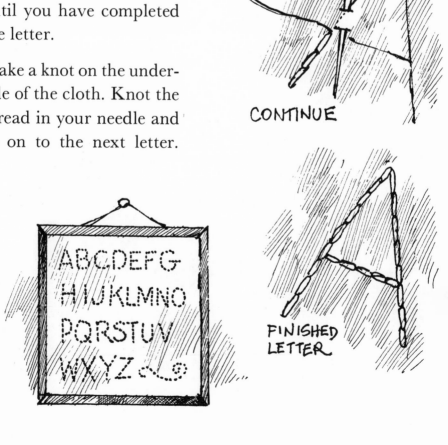

BEGIN

CONTINUE

FINISHED LETTER

ABCDEFG
HIJKLMNO
PQRSTUV
WXYZ

Pioneer Models and Dioramas

Trencher

The early settlers ate their food from wooden trenchers. A trencher was a slab of wood that had been hollowed out on one side. Two people ate from each trencher. They ate with their fingers mostly, or if the food could not be managed with fingers, they used a wooden spoon. There were no table forks in those days.

To make models of a trencher and wooden spoon:

1. Press a small amount of salt clay into a rectangular shape. With your fingers press in the center to make it rounded.

2. Shape another small bit of salt clay into a spoon.

3. Let the clay dry and paint the trencher and spoon.

Spinning Wheel

Spinning means twisting. And for the early-settler woman, spinning the wool and flax into thread was a never-ending task. Hour after hour was spent in turning the spinning wheel to make thread.

You can find out about spinning, though, without a spinning wheel. Take a piece of cotton and pull away a bit of it. Start twisting it into a thread. Keep pulling and twisting. See how long it takes to make a long smooth thread? The spinning wheel could do it much, much faster. It was truly a time saver for the early settler.

To make a model of a spinning wheel:

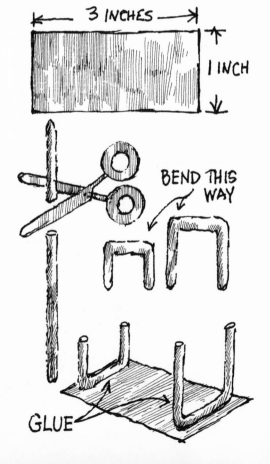

1. Cut a piece of cardboard three inches long and one inch wide.

2. Cut two inches from the end of a pipe cleaner. Bend this as shown in the picture to make a set of legs. Then bend the longer piece of pipe cleaner in the same way to make longer legs for the other end. Glue the legs in place at each end of the cardboard.

3. Cut a circle about the size of a fifty-cent piece from cardboard. Make a small hole in the center of the circle.

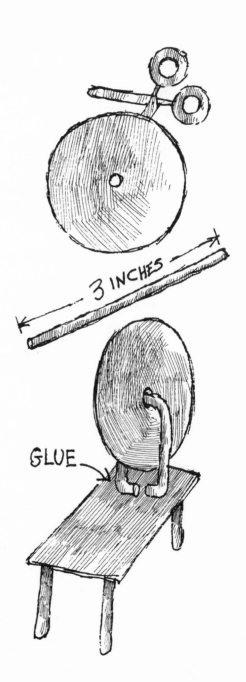

4. Cut a piece of pipe cleaner three inches long. Fold it in half. Slip the cardboard circle on one end and slide it up to the middle of the pipe cleaner. Bend each end of the pipe cleaner just a little. Glue this in place at the lower end of the cardboard stand.

5. Cut another piece of pipe cleaner three inches long. Bend it into a horseshoe shape. Cut a piece of pipe cleaner long enough to go across the top of this with a little left over on each side. Twist this piece in place around the ends of the horseshoe shape. Glue the rounded end of the horseshoe shape in place at the higher end of the platform.

6. Paint the spinning wheel.

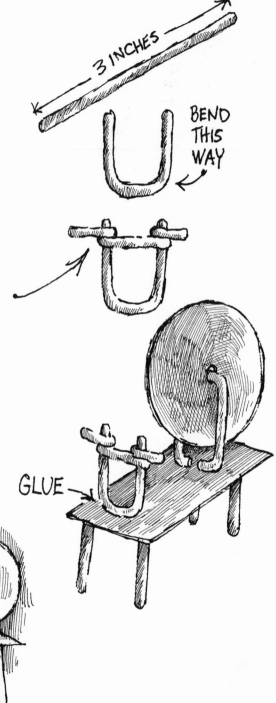

3 INCHES

BEND THIS WAY

GLUE

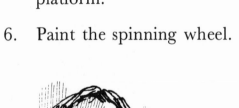

Making Dyes

The early settlers not only had to spin their own thread and weave their own cloth, they also had to make their own dyes and dye the cloth. They used the bark from trees, certain plant roots, and other things from nature to make their dyes.

You can make dyes too. Perhaps the colors will not be as bright and clear as you are used to seeing, but you can see how it was done. You may want to try some experiments and find your own ways to make colors.

Here are some ways to make dye.

Yellow
1. Collect the dry outside skins of onions. Pour hot tap water over them. Let them soak overnight. Strain off the liquid. Throw away the skins.

Purple
2. Bottled unsweetened grape juice makes a nice shade of purple.

Red

3. Beets make a light shade of red. Grate or grind raw beets in a food chopper. Put the pulp in a piece of cloth and squeeze out the juice.

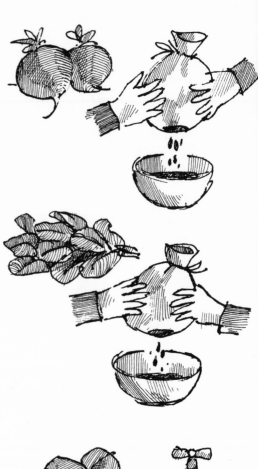

Green

4. A light shade of green can be gotten by grinding fresh spinach or green grass in a food grinder. After grinding, put the pulp in a piece of cloth and squeeze out the juice.

Brown

5. Black walnut hulls (not the shell) make a dark brown. Pound the hulls off the nuts and put them in a pan. Pour hot tap water over the hulls and let them soak overnight. Strain off the liquid and throw away the hulls.

Dyeing Your Costume

You may want to dye some of the projects you've made, such as your costume, with your dyes.

1. Put the dye in a pan or bowl large enough to hold the cloth you want to dye.

2. Wet the cloth before you put it in the dye.

3. Add enough warm water to the dye to cover the cloth.

4. Stir the cloth so it will dye evenly. Try to keep it under the water. Let it stay in the dye for fifteen or twenty minutes.

5. Rinse the dyed cloth just a little in cold water. Hang it up to dry.

Half-faced Shelter

When a young man and his bride set out to make a new home, they took with them only what could be packed on a horse. Of course they had to have tools—an ax for felling trees, a hoe to start crops. A woman had to have a big cooking pot and perhaps a long-handled skillet. Another important item was corn to be used as food and for planting their own crops. The young couple traveled until they found a place to their liking. They wanted land that was flat and fertile, and they had to have water nearby. Usually they didn't have to travel too far to meet their needs. Land was plentiful in the very early days.

The man's first task in settling new land was to make a shelter. He felled young trees and quickly put up a half-faced camp. The sides were built of logs. The top was covered with bark, and the whole front was open.

To make a model of a half-faced shelter:

1. Cut a square of cardboard. Then cut the square in half to form two triangles.

2. Cut a piece of cardboard the length of the long side of the triangles and as wide as you want the roof to be.

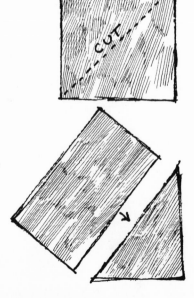

3. Tape the long sides of the triangles to the roof on the inside and outside.

4. Cut logs from soda straws the length you need them to cover the sides of the shelter. Glue them in place.

5. From a paper bag, cut a piece of paper a little larger than the roof. Paint the paper brown. Let it dry.

6. Cut the paper into short strips to represent bark. Glue the strips of bark to the roof. Have the strips overlap a little.

7. Paint the sides of the shelter.

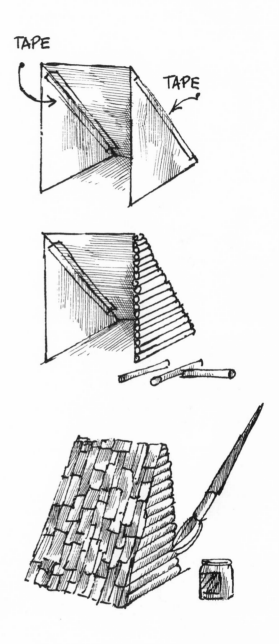

Cooking Rack

A fire was built in front of the camp. The fire was kept burning all the time. There were no matches in those days and it was very hard to start a fire with flint and steel. The fire gave them warmth and light. It kept away wild animals and cooked their food. A cooking rack was made from which the woman could hang her big iron pot.

Perhaps you would like to make a cooking rack to go in front of your half-faced shelter.

1. Find two sticks that are crotched at one end. Be sure they are as long as you want your cooking rack to be high. Put a ball of salt clay around the straight end of each to make a base.

2. Stand the sticks a few inches apart. Lay a straight stick across the top, letting it rest in the crotches.

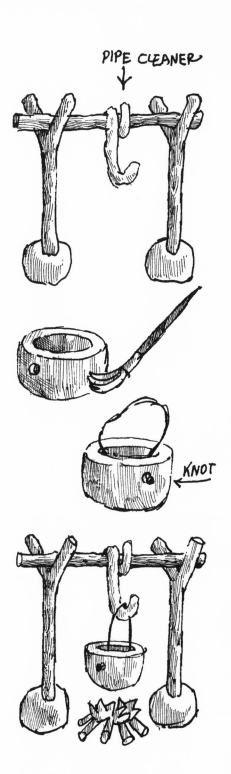

3. Wrap a piece of pipe cleaner around the middle of the cross stick. Shape the end into a hook to hold a pot.

4. Make a pot from salt clay. Put a hole in each side. When the pot dries, paint it.

5. Make a handle for the pot by putting a thread through the holes and tying a tight knot in each end.

6. Slip the pot handle over the pipe cleaner hook.

7. Make a fire by using twigs for wood and bits of painted salt clay for the flame.

Diorama-Half-faced Camp

A diorama is like a miniature stage setting. The background is painted and models are used to set the scene. Through dioramas you can get a better idea of the way things really looked in the days of the early settlers.

Cardboard cartons make fine frames for dioramas. The size you need will depend upon the size of your models and how much you want to show in your diorama.

There are many dioramas you can make with the models from this book.

Paint a river or a stream in the background. Add models of the half-faced shelter, the cooking rack and fire. Model a horse from salt clay. You may also want to model some wild animals. Deer, raccoon, panthers, bears, and even buffalo were in the forest in Daniel Boone's days.

Model Trees

And of course you will need trees. To make trees:

1. Find sticks as long as you want the trees to be high.

2. Cut strips of cotton. Sprinkle one side of the cotton with glue. Place a stick at one end of the glued side. Roll the cotton around the stick. Let the glue dry.

    GLUE

    ← COTTON

3. Paint the trees.

4. Make a base for the trees with salt clay.

    SALT CLAY
    ← BASE

Pipe Cleaner People

You may want to make people to go with your models. Pipe cleaners are very good for this.

1. To form the head, make a loop in one end of a pipe cleaner, starting about two inches from the top. Twist the end around the main piece to fasten. For the body, make a larger loop with the other end of the pipe cleaner and twist the end in place just below the loop for the head.

2. Cut two pieces of pipe cleaner for arms and two for legs. Twist them in place on the body.

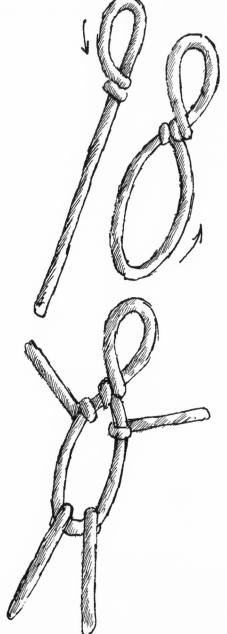

3. Cut two pieces of cloth or paper large enough to fit the head and two more for the body. Glue a piece on each side of the head and body.

4. Glue cotton on the head for hair. Let the glue dry.

5. Paint the doll's skin and hair the color you want them to be.

6. Glue or tie on clothes.

Log Cabin

Of course a half-faced camp would not do for cold weather. So the man immediately started cutting logs for a proper cabin. When he had cut seventy or eighty he asked all the neighbors to a log raising. They came from miles around bringing their axes and often their own food. They stayed for several days, camping out at night.

The early cabins had one room, and packed earth often served as a floor. If the cabin had any windows, they were just open holes or covered with oiled paper. Oiled paper let more light through.

To make a model of a log cabin:

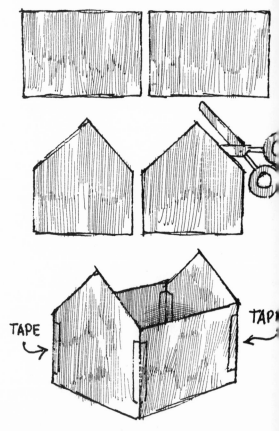

1. Cut two pieces of cardboard of equal size to make the front and back of the cabin.

2. Cut two other pieces a bit narrower and about one inch higher to make the sides. Cut the extra inch into a peak as shown in the picture.

3. Tape the front and back to the sides to make the frame.

TAPE

TAP

4. Draw the door and windows (if you want them). Cut along one side and the top of the door. Open it to the inside. Cut along the top and bottom of the windows. Then cut down through the center. Open them to the outside for shutters.

5. For the chimney, cut four strips of cardboard a little higher than the cabin from the peak to the bottom. The side strips should be half as wide as the front and back strips. Tape the sides to the front and back to make the frame. Glue the chimney frame onto one side of the cabin frame. Let the glue dry.

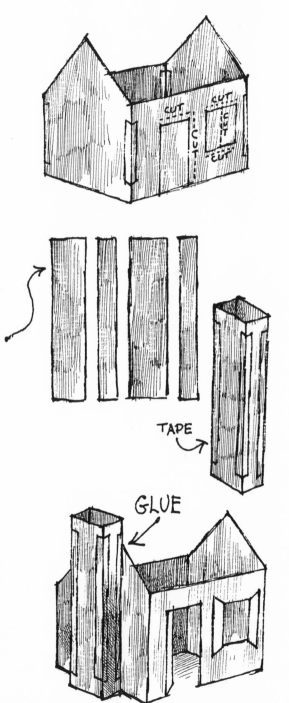

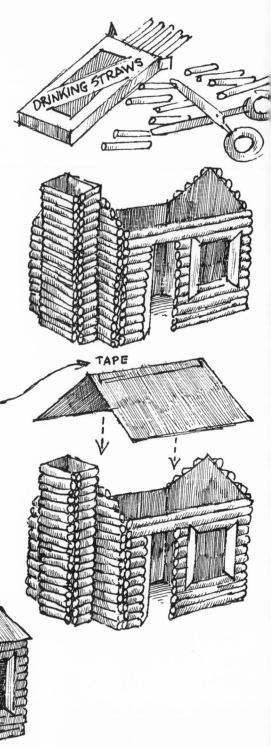

6. Cut soda straws the length you need them for logs. Glue the logs in place on the cabin frame. Continue doing this until the frame and the chimney are covered. Let the glue dry.

7. For the roof, cut two pieces of cardboard large enough to reach from the peak to the edge of the frame on one side. Tape the pieces together in the center.

8. With the tape on the underside, fit the roof on the cabin. Tape it in place from the inside.

Quern

A quern was made of two flat circular stones. It was used for grinding corn into meal. The lower stone was fixed in place. The upper stone had a funnel-shaped hole in the center. The corn was poured into this. There was a handle on one side to turn the top stone. As the stone was turned the corn was ground into meal.

To make a model of a quern:

1. Take a piece of salt clay and press it flat with your hand. Use a small glass to cut out one stone. Then make another stone the same size.

2. Put one stone aside to dry as it is. It will be the bottom stone. In the other make a funnel-shaped opening in the center. Stick a short stick in one side of the top for the turning handle.

3. Let the clay dry and paint the quern.

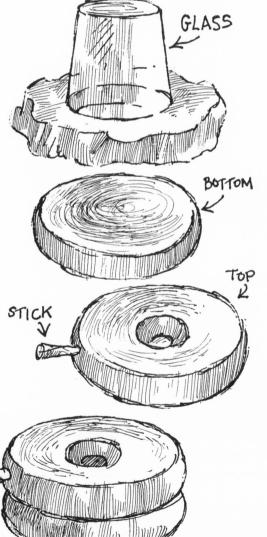

GLASS

BOTTOM

STICK

TOP

Well and Sweep

As soon as a man had time, he dug a well and put up a sweep. The sweep was a long pole lying in the crotch of a post. The sweep made it easier to lift full buckets of water from the well.

Perhaps you would like to make a well and a sweep.

1. Use a small round bottle such as the ones pills come in. Shape salt clay around the bottom, for a base. If you want a stone well, press small pebbles into the clay. Let the clay dry.

2. Find a stick about twice as high as the well that is crotched at one end. Put a ball of salt clay around the straight end to make a base.

3. Find a straight stick about twice as long as the crotched stick. Wrap a piece of pipe cleaner around one end of the straight stick. Shape the end of the pipe cleaner to make a hook.

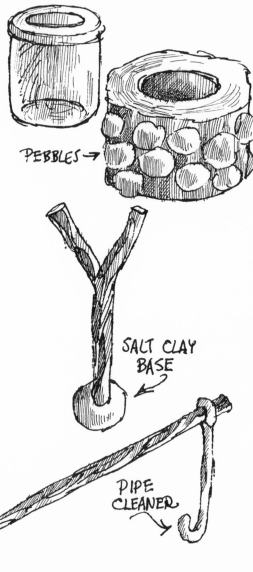

PEBBLES →

SALT CLAY BASE ↙

PIPE CLEANER ↓

4. Lay the stick across the crotched stick so that the hook hangs over the well.

5. Shape a bucket from aluminum foil. Put a small hole in each side. Make a handle for the bucket by putting a string through the holes and tying a tight knot at each end. Slip the handle of the bucket over the hook.

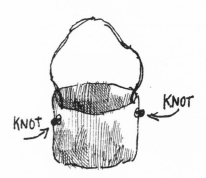

Diorama-Log Cabin

Paint a forest background. Add models of the log cabin, the well and sweep, and the quern. Model some tree stumps from salt clay and place them around to show where trees were chopped down.

You may want to make a fence around your cabin. Because there was so much land the early settlers didn't worry about wasting space. Their fences zigzagged all over the place. For this reason they were called worm fences.

Worm Fence

To make a worm fence:

1. Cut soda straws into the lengths you plan to use as logs.

2. Lay the first two logs so that they form a V with the end of one across the end of the other. Glue the crisscrossed ends in place.

3. Continue laying V's with the ends crisscrossing until you have fenced in the part you want.

4. Go back and start the next row on top of the first, always gluing the ends of the logs in place. Continue building in this way until the fence is as high as you want it to be.

5. Let the glue dry and paint the fence.

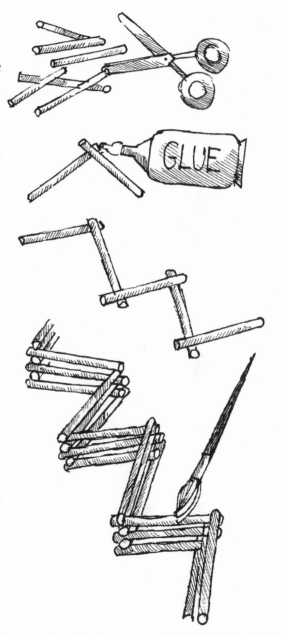

Table and Bench

The furniture in the cabin was very simple and there was not much of it. A tree stump often served as a chair. The table was a rough slab of wood set on four posts. Benches were made the same way, only narrower and lower. Nails were very scarce. The furniture was pegged together with wooden pegs.

You may want to make furniture for a cabin.

1. Cut two pieces of pipe cleaner of equal length to make the table legs. Bend them as shown in the picture.

2. Cut a piece of cardboard the size you want the table to be. Glue a set of legs at each end of the cardboard.

3. Make the bench the same way, only narrower and with shorter legs.

4. Let the glue dry and paint the table and bench.

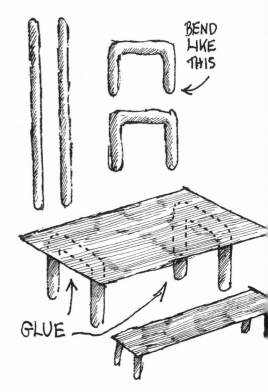

BEND LIKE THIS

GLUE

Clothing Rack

The log cabin had no closets. Extra clothing was hung on pegs.

To make a clothing rack:

1. Cut a strip of cardboard. Make a row of small holes in it.

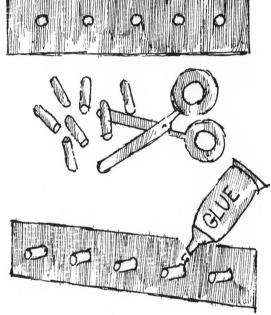

2. Cut short pieces of pipe cleaner. Put a piece in each hole and glue it in place.

3. Glue or tape the clothes rack to a side of the box.

Fireplace

A big fireplace was sure to be found in every log cabin. All of the cooking was done in the fireplace. It also furnished the heat and a part of the light for the cabin.

To make a fireplace for your diorama:

1. At one end of the carton, on the outside, draw where you think the fireplace should be. Cut along the top line and the bottom line. Cut down through the center.

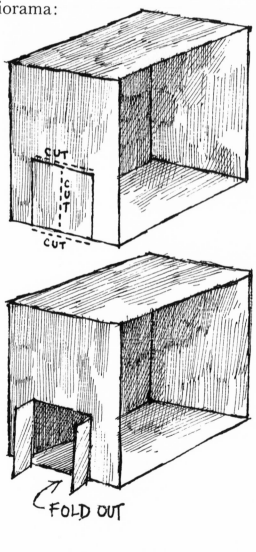

2. Fold out the side pieces. Cut other pieces of cardboard for the back, top, and bottom. Tape them to the side pieces.

3. Make a small hole in each side of the fireplace. Find a stick long enough to reach across the fireplace. Put this through the holes for a cooking rod. Wrap a piece of pipe cleaner around the middle of the stick. Shape the end as a hook to hold a cooking pot.

4. Shape a cooking pot from salt clay. Put a hole in each side. When the clay dries, paint the pot.

5. Make a handle for the pot by putting thread through the holes and tying a tight knot in each end. Slip the pot handle over the pipe cleaner hook.

6. Make a fire by using twigs for logs and bits of painted salt clay for flame.

INSIDE VIEW

Beds

The beds were just as simply made. The frame was made from poles and split planks were laid across the poles. The mattress was stuffed with cornhusks or dried leaves.

In order to save space a lower bed that would fit under the higher bed was made for the children. The high bed was called a jack bed, the low one a trundle bed. The trundle bed could be pulled out at night and pushed back under the bed and out of the way during the day.

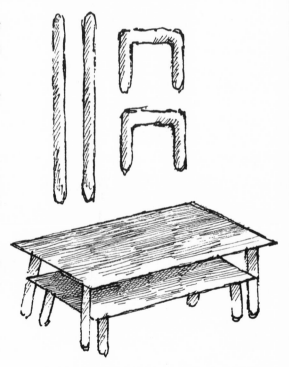

1. Cut two pieces of pipe cleaner of equal lengths for the legs of the jack bed. Bend them as shown in the picture.

2. Cut a piece of cardboard the size you want the bed to be. Glue a set of legs to each end of the cardboard.

3. Make the trundle bed the same way, only smaller and with shorter legs.

4. Let the glue dry and paint the beds.

5. Perhaps you would like to make mattresses for the beds. If so, follow the instructions in step 6 for making a cradle mattress (page 40).

Diorama-Inside of a Log Cabin

Paint the cabin as you think it should be. Add the models of the beds, table, bench, and spinning wheel.

Diorama- School Room

Paint the walls of the box to look like logs. Either paint or make a fireplace at one end. (See "Fireplace," steps 1, 2, and 6, page 82.) Make several long benches. Make a table and a small bench for the teacher. (See "Table and Bench," page 80.) Place the table and teacher's bench at one end of the room. Arrange the long benches in two rows. Shape a water bucket and dipper from salt clay. Cut some miniature hornbooks from paper and place them on the benches.

You may also want to make pipe-cleaner children for your schoolroom.

Fort

The early settlers had many dangers to face in this new land. One of the biggest dangers came from hostile Indians. Wherever there was a settlement there was usually a fort nearby.

The early forts were nothing more than four log walls with a tall blockhouse, used as a shooting tower, at each corner. When there was danger of an Indian attack the settlers moved their families and animals into the fort.

To make a model of a fort:

1. Cut four strips of cardboard the length and height you want the walls to be. Fold under one-fourth inch at the ends of each strip. In one strip draw a door. Cut it along one side and the top. Open the door to the inside.

2. The blockhouses should be about twice as high as the wall. To make the frames, see "Log Cabin," steps 1, 2, 3 on page 72 and step 7 on page 74. Make four of these frames.

3. In two adjoining sides of each frame cut a small slit for shooting through. Cut a door in one of the other sides.

4. Arrange the blockhouses so that the slits are facing the outside. Tape the folded ends of the wall strips to the sides of the blockhouses to make the frame for the fort. Tape the inside and the outside.

5. Cut soda straws the length you need them for logs. Glue the logs in place on the walls and the blockhouses. Let the glue dry and paint the fort.

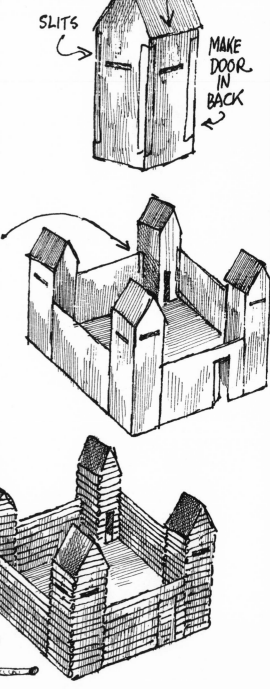

SLITS

MAKE DOOR IN BACK

Diorama-Fort

Paint a background of trees with a cabin here and there. Place the model of the fort in the center of the box. Leave a clearing around the fort, but scatter some trees along the background. You may want to dress some pipe cleaner people as Indians and place them among the trees. You may also want to make a couple of small log cabins to put inside the fort for the people to stay in. And of course you will need to model some salt clay animals to put inside the fort.

Covered Wagon

When an early settler moved his family, often they traveled in a covered wagon. Many covered wagons traveled together in a long line called a wagon train. They never knew what dangers they might meet. It was safer to travel in a crowd.

To make a model of a covered wagon:

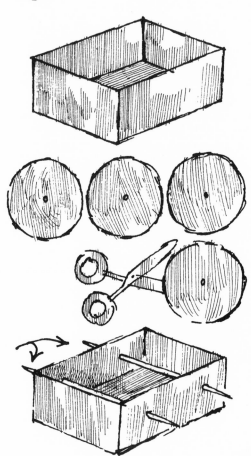

1. Use a small box to make the body. A match or paper clip box is fine.

2. Using a nickel for a pattern, draw four circles on a piece of cardboard. Cut out the circles. Make a small hole in the center of each.

3. Make a small hole on each side of the body of the wagon about a half inch from the corner. Stick a toothpick through the hole on each side so that it goes through the hole on the opposite side.

4. Put a cardboard circle on the ends of each toothpick for wheels. Glue the wheels in place.

5. Stick two toothpicks into the front of the wagon to make the shaft. Paint the wagon and let the paint dry.

6. Use three pipe cleaners to make the frame for the cover. Fit them inside the body of the wagon at the back, front, and middle. Glue the ends in place.

7. Cut a strip of white cloth long enough to reach from the top of the wheels across the frame and two inches longer than the length of the body of the wagon.

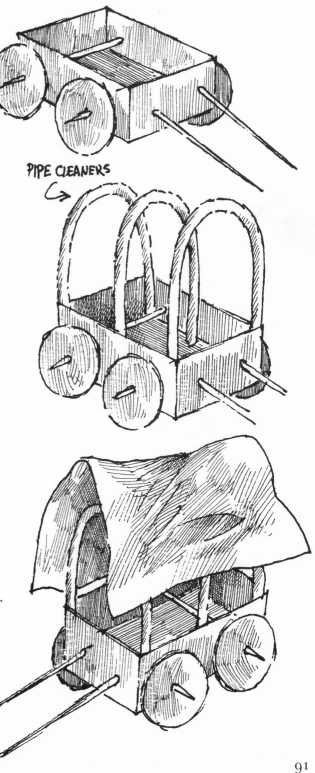

PIPE CLEANERS

8. Fold a one-fourth-inch hem on each end to make a casing for a drawstring. Sew the hems down. Stitch close to the inside edge.

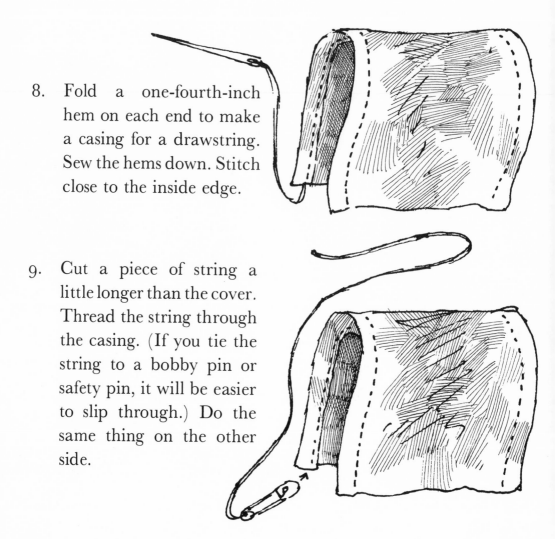

9. Cut a piece of string a little longer than the cover. Thread the string through the casing. (If you tie the string to a bobby pin or safety pin, it will be easier to slip through.) Do the same thing on the other side.

10. Lay the cover across the frame. Glue the sides in place on the body of the wagon. Pull the drawstrings to make the cover fit snugly. Tie them into a bow.

11. Model a horse from salt clay. Let the clay dry, and paint the horse. Glue bits of string or yarn to make a mane and tail.

12. Fasten the horse between the shafts with string. Make some string reins and tie or glue them to the horse.

Flatboat

As the land became crowded along the eastern coast people began to seek new lands farther west. Some of the early settlers traveled by water. They built flatboats and loaded all their things on them. They floated the flatboats downstream on a river. The settlers made their boats as comfortable as they could. Sometimes they lived on them for as much as a year while they cleared land and built a cabin.

The back half of the flatboat was fenced off and used as a yard for the animals. The front half was used as a yard for the family.

You can make a model of a flatboat with the top of a box. A shoebox does nicely.

1. Make a small log cabin. Glue it in place across the center of the box top. (See directions for making a log cabin, pages 72–74.)

2. Make a fence of soda straws from the cabin to the edge of the boat.

STRAW FENCE

3. Cut a piece of paper about three inches wide and three inches long to make the blade of the steering oar. Fold the paper in half. Put glue on one side of the inside.

Lay the soda straw inside the fold. Press the glued paper together around it.

4. Bend a small piece of pipe cleaner into a horseshoe shape. Glue this at one end of the boat to make the oar lock.

5. Paint the flatboat.

6. Model a cow, a horse, and some chickens from salt clay.

7. Make a small pile of dried grass as a haystack to feed the animals.

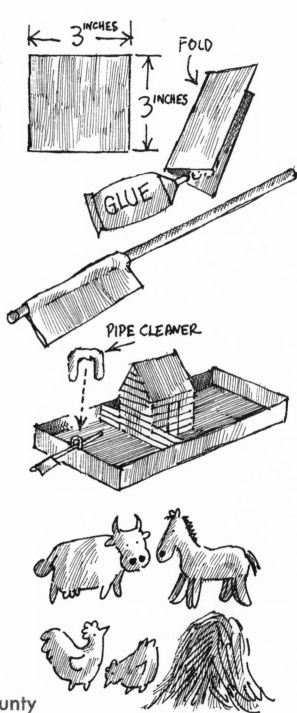

Diorama-Flatboat

Paint the bottom of the carton as a river. Paint in a background of hills and trees.